Hamsters
A to Z

Lorraine Hill

T.F.H. Publications, Inc.
One TFH Plaza
Third and Union Avenues
Neptune City, NJ 07753

This book has been published with the intent to provide accurate and authoritative information in regard to the subject matter within. While every precaution has been taken in preparation of this book, the publisher and author assume no responsibility for errors or omissions. Neither is any liability assumed for damages resulting from the use of the information herein.

ISBN 0-7938-3112-1

Contents

Introduction

The hamster is the most popular of the rodents that are commonly kept as pets in many countries today. This book explores how hamsters became part of our lives and how we can best understand and care for them.

What Are Hamsters?

Hamsters are mammals and are members of the order *Rodentia*. All rodents have two large teeth in the center of their top and bottom jaws that continually grow, meaning that these animals have to gnaw to prevent their teeth from overgrowing. The word "rodent" is derived from the Latin word *rodere*, which means "to gnaw."

Rodentia is scientifically divided into various families and subfamilies. Hamsters belong to a subfamily known as *Cricetidae,* meaning "burrowers." In the wild, hamsters inhabit burrows consisting of tunnels and chambers.

The subfamily *Cricetidae* is further divided into genera (the plural of genus), and the species of hamsters kept as pets fall into three separate genera—*Mesocricetus,* meaning "middle-sized hamster"; *Phodopus,* meaning "short-tailed dwarf hamster"; and *Cricetulus,* meaning "rat-like hamster."

There are five species of hamsters that are commonly kept as pets, and in order of availability and popularity they are the Syrian hamster, the Dwarf Campbells Russian hamster, the Dwarf Winter White Russian hamster, the Chinese hamster, and the Roborovski hamster.

There are several different species of dwarf hamster, all of which are smaller than the Syrian hamster.

> **A is for Alien Hamster**–This is another name sometimes given to the hairless Syrian hamster because of its bizarre appearance.

The Syrian hamster is the largest hamster kept as a pet and is a species of the *Mesocricetus* genus. The Dwarf Campbells Russian, Dwarf Winter White Russian, and Roborovski are collectively known as dwarf hamsters and

Scientific Names

Syrian hamster—*Mesocricetus auratus*

Dwarf Campbells Russian hamster—*Phodopus campbelli*

Dwarf Winter White Russian hamster—*Phodopus sunogris*

Roborovski hamster—*Phodopus Roborovskii*

Chinese hamster—*Cricetulus griseus*

belong to the genus *Phodopus,* while the Chinese hamster belongs to the genus *Cricetulus.* Although the Chinese hamster is not technically a dwarf hamster, it is often referred to as such because of its small size.

All hamster species have expandable cheek pouches, although the Syrian hamster makes more use of them than the other species. By placing items in the cheek pouches, the hamster can collect food and bedding material during his travels and take them back to his burrow. On his return home, he will empty the contents from his pouches by pushing the food and bedding out through his mouth to build a food store and nest. Hamsters are natural hoarders, and the name hamster is derived from the German word *hamstern,* which means "to hoard." Hoarding food ensures that the hamster has something to eat when food outside the burrow may be scarce. A full-grown Syrian hamster can carry up to half his own body weight in grain in his cheek pouches at one time.

The Syrian hamster leads a solitary life, each with his own burrow that he will fiercely defend against other hamsters. The dwarf hamsters and the Chinese hamster, however, are sociable and live in pairs or groups, although they will attack strangers that wander into their territory.

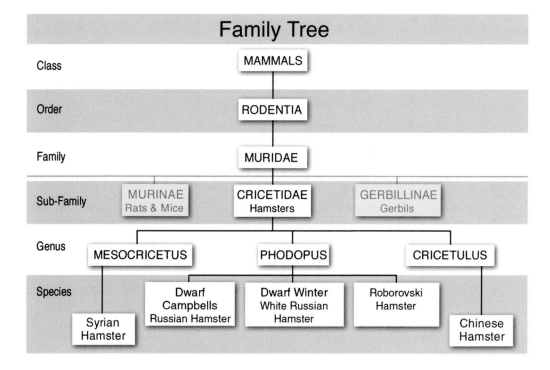

Hamster Behavior

Staring Into Space—When a hamster has smelled or heard something that is unfamiliar, he will stand completely still on his hind legs with a vacant expression on his face. The hamster listens intently for signs of danger but does not bring attention to himself by moving. He is ready to flee if he senses danger.

Sudden Squeal—A hamster will let out a short squeal if he is surprised or frightened.

Continuous Squealing—An extremely nervous hamster will squeal continuously. Sometimes the hamster may stand on his hind legs, raise his paws, and squeal. This indicates that the hamster is extremely frightened of something nearby that he senses is dangerous.

Side Rubbing—Syrian hamsters have a scent gland located on each hip that they use to mark their territory. The glands on male hamsters are more pronounced and look like a mole. At times, the glands may be sticky. Many hamsters rub their sides around their cage after it has just been cleaned in order to lay their scent down again.

Teeth Chattering—A hamster will grind his teeth when he is annoyed. This is a "leave me alone" warning.

Fighting—Serious fighting between hamsters can cause injury or even death. Syrian hamsters are solitary once mature, and whether they are left together from a young age or introduced to another when they are older, serious fighting will occur. Fighting may occur with dwarf hamsters even though they are sociable. This fighting usually only occurs when introducing two older hamsters to each other or when something has deeply upset an established pair.

Squabbling—Dwarf hamsters, although sociable, do squabble. This squabbling helps to establish the dominance hierarchy within a pair or group. A dominant hamster will often chase others and corner them in order to assert his dominance over them. The cornered hamster will often squeal, stand on his hind legs, and "box" at the dominant hamster or raise his arms. Once the dominant hamster is satisfied that the cornered hamster has submitted, he will smell the belly and sometimes lick his belly to reassure him. Dwarf hamsters recognize each other by their smell.

Fleeing and Burrowing—A hamster that senses danger will often flee rather than face the source of danger. Therefore, a frightened hamster will often flee in a frenzy around his cage or attempt to burrow frantically in order to avoid any danger.

Investigation and Burrowing—Hamsters are naturally inquisitive and, when placed in a new environment, will often spend much time investigating and attempting to burrow.

Carrying Food—It is natural for a hamster to carry food in his cheek pouches to take to his food store. However, if a hamster constantly carries food in his pouches and does not empty them, this is a sign that he feels insecure and uncomfortable in his environment. When frightened, the hamster may empty his pouches where he stands in order to make fleeing easier.

Hamsters mainly inhabit semi-desert areas and are nocturnal, sleeping in their burrows during the hot days and emerging in the cooler evenings to spend the night foraging for food. Their eyesight is poor and they rely mainly on their extremely acute senses of smell, hearing, and touch.

Hamsters have scent glands that they use to mark their territory, and in the case of dwarf hamsters, the scent is also used to recognize other hamsters within the group.

Their hearing is very sensitive, and they can hear sounds beyond the human range.

B **is for Banana**—A favorite treat for many hamsters.

History

Although the Syrian hamster is the most readily available hamster today, it was not the first of the pet hamster species to be discovered. The Dwarf Winter White Russian hamster hails from Siberia, where it lives on grass steppes and was first recorded in 1770.

In 1797, the Syrian hamster was discovered for the first time but was not named as a new species until 1839, when George Robert Waterhouse captured it. Originally, the Syrian hamster was named the Golden hamster because of its natural golden-brown coloring, but this was later changed to the Syrian hamster when new color mutations began to emerge. A group of Syrian hamsters was brought from Syria to the United Kingdom in 1880, but it is believed that descendants of these hamsters did not survive past 1910.

The Roborovski hamster lives among the sand dunes in the desert areas of the former Soviet Union, Mongolia, and China, and was first discovered in 1894 by Lieutenant Roborovsky, after whom it was named.

The Dwarf Winter White Russian hamster comes from Siberia, where it was first recorded in 1770.

The Chinese hamster, which, not surprisingly, comes from China, was discovered in 1900 and was frequently mistaken for other species of similar appearance. Following its discovery, it was widely used in laboratories, but breeding colonies were difficult to maintain due to the aggressive nature of pregnant females toward their mates.

C is for Cheek Pouches– These are expandable pouches on either side of the face that the hamster uses to collect and carry food back to his nest.

The Dwarf Campbells Russian hamster comes from Central Asia, where it lives in semi-desert areas and was discovered in 1905 by Thomas Campbell, after whom it is named. After its discovery, members of this species were kept at an institute in Moscow.

The Roborovski hamster lives among the sand dunes in the desert areas of the former Soviet Union, Mongolia, and China.

In 1930, Saul Alder, a parasitologist at the Hebrew University of Jerusalem, having been unsuccessful at raising Chinese hamsters for laboratory research, asked Israel Aharoni to obtain another species of hamster from the Middle East. In April 1930, Israel Ahorani located a female Syrian hamster and her young in Aleppo, Syria, and captured the group. The female immediately started to kill her young, so she was destroyed and the youngsters were hand-reared. After an escape, nine babies were recaptured and passed to the Hebrew University of Jerusalem, whereupon five more escaped and were never recovered. The remaining four were bred, and the captive population increased. Syrian hamsters were distributed in the UK in 1931, and it is believed that they were first imported into the United States in 1938. A relatively short time after their importation, they were obtained by enthusiasts and emerged onto the pet markets of the UK and US.

In 1963, the Dwarf Campbells Russian hamster was exported to a UK zoo and was later used in laboratories.

In the 1960s, the Dwarf Winter White Russian was kept and bred as a laboratory animal in Germany. Most of the hamsters of this species kept as pets today are descended from this stock. Also in the 1960s, the Chinese hamster was introduced to the pet market but never enjoyed the popularity of the Syrian hamster. This may have been due to the difficulty in maintaining breeding colonies or to its more mouselike appearance.

It appears that the Roborovski hamster was first kept in captivity within the USSR sometime after 1970.

D is for Djungarian—Another name given to the Dwarf Winter White Russian hamster, after the region in which it lives in the wild.

Chinese hamsters like these were discovered in 1900 in China.

In the 1970s, UK hamster fanciers obtained pairs of Dwarf Campbells Russian hamsters from the zoos, and the Dwarf Winter White Russian was introduced into UK laboratories. In the late 1970s, the Dwarf Campbells Russian hamster and the Dwarf Winter White Russian hamster were introduced into the UK and US pet markets. The Roborovski hamster was imported into the UK, but unfortunately it did not breed.

Captures of wild Syrian hamsters have since occurred in 1968, 1971, 1978, and 1980, and some of these hamsters were taken to the US, although it is unclear whether any of their descendants ended up for sale as pets.

The Roborovski hamster was later imported into some European countries, and these were then reintroduced into the UK pet market in 1990. In 1998, Roborovski hamsters were imported by US hamster enthusiasts and are now breeding in captivity.

Hamsters in Research

This section will not discuss the ethics of animals in research, but it is important to know about the significance of the hamster in the laboratory over the years.

By 1971, the hamster was the third most common animal used in research laboratories. The vast majority of these hamsters were Syrian hamsters, although the Chinese and a few other species that are not kept as pets were also used.

The Chinese has been used in laboratory research for many years, but the tendency of the females to become aggressive toward the males, particularly when the females are pregnant, makes it difficult to maintain breeding colonies. It is this problem that led to the capture of the Syrian hamster in 1930, which later led to the introduction of the Syrian hamster

In 1905, Thomas Campbell discovered the Dwarf Campbells Russian hamster in the semi-desert areas of Central Asia.

E **is for European Black Bear**—or "black bear," another name sometimes given to the black Syrian hamster.

into the pet market. The Syrian hamster became a popular animal for use in research due to its mild temperament, quick reproduction, its freedom from natural diseases, and the ease with which researchers could induce disease in the species.

Syrian hamsters have also been used for research into tumors. The early hairless Syrian hamsters were found to be prone to skin cancers and have been used to carry out research into this disease. The Syrian hamster's tendency to hibernate when there is a sudden drop in temperature has also allowed research into hypothermia to be carried out.

More recently, the Syrian hamster has been found to have a high tolerance for alcohol and has been used in research into curbing alcohol addiction. (Of course, a high tolerance for alcohol should not be interpreted as meaning that giving alcohol to a pet hamster is beneficial. Alcohol is harmful to hamsters and should not be given to them.)

The Chinese hamster has been used for researching infectious diseases, and in 1957, the occurrence of diabetes in Chinese hamsters facilitated important diabetes research. Much research today is carried out using cultivated cells and ova from Chinese hamsters. Chinese hamster cells have also been used for research into reproduction, cancers, disease mutations, and the effects of radiation.

Many pet hamsters of all species today descend from the original wild-caught specimens that were used as laboratory animals.

Both the Syrian and Chinese hamster have been used in parasitic research as well as viral research such as influenza and measles.

Other species of hamster that are not kept as pets have been used for research into smoke inhalation and respiratory tumors.

In many European countries today the number of animals used in research is declining, but it is unclear whether the same is true in the US.

Syrian hamsters have been popular pets since the mid-20th century.

Vital Statistics

Syrian Hamster
Adult Length: 6 to 8 inches (15 to 20 cm)
Adult Weight: 5 to 7 ounces (140 to 200 grams)
Adult Food Consumption: 1/3 to 1/2 ounce (10 to 15 grams) dry food per day
Adult Water Consumption: 6 teaspoons (30 ml) per day

Dwarf Campbells Russian Hamster
Adult Length: 4 to 5 inches (10 to 12 cm)
Adult Weight: 1.5 to 2 ounces (40 to 60 grams)
Adult Food Consumption: 1/4 to 1/2 ounce (7 to 15 grams) dry food per day
Adult Water Consumption: 2 1/2 to 3 teaspoons (12 to 15 ml) per day

Dwarf Winter White Russian Hamster
Adult Length: 3 to 4 inches (8 to 10 cm)
Adult Weight: 1.5 to 2 ounces (40 to 60 grams)
Adult Food Consumption: 1/4 to 1/2 ounce (7 to 15 grams) dry food per day
Adult Water Consumption: 2 1/2 to 3 teaspoons (12 to 15 ml) per day

Chinese Hamster
Adult Length: 4 to 5 inches (10 to 12 cm)
Adult Weight: 1.5 to 1.8 ounces (40 to 50 grams)
Adult Food Consumption: 1/4 to 1/2 ounce (7 to 15 grams) dry food per day
Adult Water Consumption: 2 1/2 to 3 teaspoons (12 to 15 ml) per day

Roborovski Hamster
Adult Length: 1.5 to 2 inches (4 to 5 cm)
Adult Weight: 1 to 1.5 ounces (25 to 40 grams)
Adult Food Consumption: 1/4 to 2/5 ounces (7 to 12 grams) dry food per day
Adult Water Consumption: 2 to 2 1/2 teaspoons (10-12 ml) per day

The Life of a Hamster

Hamsters are born without fur after a 16-day gestation. Their skin is semi-transparent, allowing the veins and internal organs to be seen on close inspection. They are blind, with skin totally covering the eyes. The eyes can be seen through the transparent skin, especially on hamsters that are to have black eyes. The ears are partly formed and closed, meaning that the hamsters are deaf at this stage. Although they are deaf, they are vocal and able to squeak. The baby hamster is born with small teeth that aid him in gripping the mother's teats in order to feed.

Each hamster is born at approximately ten-minute intervals, and the birth is often followed by the emission of a placenta by the mother. In between the birth of each baby, a mother will often move the newborn hamster to the nest, but sometimes she will give birth to the whole litter before gathering the babies and moving them all into the nest.

A baby hamster weighs only two to three grams at birth and is approximately one-and-a-half centimeters in length—slightly more than half an inch.

This pregnant Syrian hamster will give birth after a 16-day gestation.

One Day Old

After birth, the babies begin to suckle. Often, the milk they drink is visible through their semi-transparent skin as a white mass in the stomach. The baby hamster becomes noticeably stronger and wriggles around more. The mother lies on the

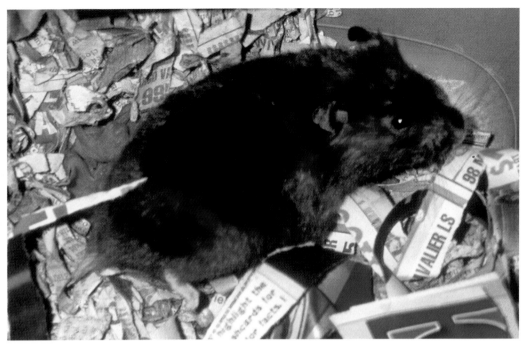

Each baby hamster is born at approximately ten-minute intervals. The mother lies on the babies to nurse them.

babies to nurse them, and when she moves away, the babies wriggle around trying to find her. On her return, they immediately begin to suckle again. Life continues this way for the first week or so.

Two to Three Days Old

The skin becomes less transparent and begins to show pigment on those babies that will develop dark skin. Not all colors result in dark skin.

Four to Five Days Old

The ears have developed and opened, allowing the baby hamsters to hear for the first time. Fur begins to develop.

Six to Ten Days Old

Short fur develops all over the body, with fine hair on the ears. The skin over the eyes begins to prepare for separation, and a barely visible line develops where the eyelids will form. The teeth are stronger, and the baby hamsters instinctively begin to nibble at solid food. By the tenth day, they are able to eat small pieces of soft solid food.

F is for Fluffy Bedding—A danger to hamsters if eaten because it does not dissolve in the stomach.

10 to 16 Days Old

The separation of the skin over the eyes continues, and slowly the eyelids open. The babies' muscles have developed, and the babies begin to wander from the nest. This often results in a prompt retrieval

These two-day-old baby hamsters will soon begin to show pigment and will grow short fur by ten days of age.

At two-and-a-half weeks of age, the baby hamsters' eyes are open and they are eating tiny amounts of solid food.

By 21 days of age, hamsters look like miniatures of their parents.

by the mother. By the 14th to 16th day, the separation of the eyelids is complete and the eyes are fully open. The babies are now able to manage small pieces of solid food, and although they are still suckling from the mother, they begin to investigate their environment further. By this time, the babies are two to four centimeters (about one or two inches) in length, depending on the species.

16 to 21 Days Old

The baby hamsters become stronger. They now eat solid food, and their rate of growth increases. At 21 days, they look like miniatures of their parents and have achieved a length of 2.5 to 7 centimeters (1 to 3 inches), depending on the species. At this time they become familiar enough with their environment to seek out alternative sources of drinking liquid (e.g., a water bottle), although they will continue to suckle from the mother if her milk is still available.

The confidence of the young hamsters has improved, and interaction between the littermates increases. In the dwarf species, this is often playing and establishment of dominance, but with Syrian hamsters, what appears to be playful fighting is the beginning of their instinctual solitude and territorial defenses.

21 to 28 Days Old

The baby hamsters become more confident, and their bodies become wider and firmer as the hamsters put on weight and develop further muscles. The young hamsters are now fully independent and do not need to nurse from the mother at this stage.

Females become fertile and show signs of coming into season, even though they continue their own growth and development.

> **G is for Gnawing**—Something a hamster must do to ensure that his continually growing teeth do not overgrow. Cage bars, wood chews, applewood, and hard dog biscuits are all suitable for a hamster to gnaw on.

28 to 35 Days Old

Males become sexually mature and attempt to mate with any responsive, available female.

35 Days to 4 Months

The young hamsters continue to grow and are achieving full adult size. The once-white teeth become permanently colored yellow, and the scent glands (on the belly of dwarf species and hips of Syrian hamsters) become more pronounced and noticeable.

The individual character of each hamster becomes stronger, and in the case of the dwarf species, the desire to establish a dominance hierarchy within the group in which it lives increases. In the case of the Syrian hamster, the solitary nature becomes stronger and the hamsters no longer tolerate the company of others. They seek to banish others from their environment by fighting, often causing serious injury or even death.

These five-week-old hamsters are already sexually mature and should be separated before they can breed.

H **is for Hoarding**—It is a hamster's natural instinct to store away food for times when it may be scarce.

Four to Six Months Old

The growth of the hamster is complete, and full size has been attained. This is the ideal time for females to mate, because they have completed their own development. Males are now highly fertile, meaning that dwarf hamsters kept in mixed-sex groups begin to produce young (with the possible exception of Roborovski hamsters where females do not begin to mate until the spring of the year following that in which they were born).

Syrian hamsters are now fiercely territorial, fighting off any other hamster they perceive as an intruder, with the exception of a receptive female entering a male's territory.

6 to 12 Months Old

The hamster's fertile period continues. With dwarf hamsters that are kept in mixed-sex pairs or groups, litter after litter is produced, and much of the hamsters' time is spent being parents.

12 to 14 Months Old

The hamster reaches middle age. Females come to the end of their fertile life and are no longer able to produce young (with the exception of the Roborovski hamster) although they

Dwarf hamsters may be kept in mixed-sex groups, although much of the hamsters' time will be spent raising litter after litter of babies.

An elderly hamster like this one may have problems with dry skin or thinning fur.

may continue to show signs of receptiveness to males. Male fertility is unaffected. The fine hair on the ears begins to disappear.

14 to 18 Months Old

The hamster moves into old age. The fur often starts to become thinner, particularly on the belly and around the hips, further revealing the scent glands. The fine hair on the ears vanishes. The skin may become drier, and the hamster becomes less active, sleeping more. The hamster may also begin to show signs of slight weight loss and develop a smaller appetite, because less energy is required for his less active lifestyle.

18 to 48 Months Old

Males become sterile and the hamster's life draws to an end. The hamster becomes more susceptible to illness and seems tired, moving slowly and sleeping much more. Hamsters usually live about two to four years if well cared for.

Average Lifespan

The average lifespan of each hamster species is given below, although occasionally it is possible for any hamster species to live to 4 or 5 years of age.

Syrian Hamster: 2 to 2.5 years

Dwarf Campbells Russian Hamster:

1.5 to 2 years

Dwarf Winter White Russian Hamster:

1.5 to 2 years

Chinese Hamster: 2 to 3 years

Roborovski Hamster: 3 to 4 years

Hamsters as Pets

Hamsters make ideal pets because they are small, inexpensive, take up little room, and generally have good temperaments. However, they still need all the commitment of any other pet, including a regular care routine, attention from their owners, and veterinary treatment when they are ill.

The different species of hamster have very different characteristics, so not all hamsters are equally suited as pets for different people.

The Syrian hamster (also known as the golden hamster, teddy bear hamster, standard hamster, or fancy hamster) is the largest of the species kept as pets and is generally very docile and easy to handle. This makes it an ideal pet for young children (under supervision) as well as older children and adults. Specific varieties of the Syrian hamster may be found under other names, such as the black bear hamster (a black Syrian hamster) or the alien hamster (a hairless Syrian hamster). The black Syrian hamster in the US is derived from European show hamsters. It has been bred for its temperament and is therefore exceptionally good-natured. The hairless Syrian hamster, while not a pet that will appeal to everyone because of its similarity to an extraterrestrial being, often makes a suitable pet for those who are allergic to other animals.

The Syrian hamster is the most popular pet hamster for children because it is large and generally easy to handle.

Dwarf hamsters are small and lively, and they do not tolerate clumsy or rough handling well. They are better pets for adults than for children.

The Dwarf Campbells Russian hamster and the Dwarf Winter White Russian hamster (also known as the Djungarian or Siberian hamster) are smaller and livelier than the Syrian hamster. Although many are of good temperament, they are less tolerant of clumsy handling and so are not generally suited to young children.

Although the two species are very similar, they are very different in character. The Dwarf Campbells Russian is much more boisterous and vocal in groups. The Dwarf Winter White Russian is generally more calm in its nature and tends to be less vocal. However, both make equally good pets.

The Chinese hamster, although small, is generally very good-natured and not prone to nipping unless really annoyed or frightened. They are very timid in nature and so can be difficult to catch. However, once they are caught they are very easily handled, because they move more slowly than the Russian species. This makes them more suitable for young children, provided that an adult shares in the responsibility of caring for the pet.

The Roborovski hamster is the smallest and liveliest of the species and is not easily handled, although it rarely bites. Roborovski hamsters are interesting to observe—these little guys really do live their lives in the fast lane! However, careful and regular handling is required from a young age in order to be able to handle these hamsters to any degree, so they are really only suited to older children and adults who have the patience to appreciate the nature of this species.

I **is for Incisors**—A hamster's continually growing central teeth in the center of the top and bottom jaws.

Syrian hamsters are solitary, so more than one hamster will require more than one cage. Although they are often displayed in pet shops living with their littermates, their solitary nature will soon develop. If they are kept with other hamsters past six to eight

Hamster Vandalism

Don't be fooled by that innocent look and those large beady eyes—any escaped hamster can become a major vandal. Given the opportunity, they can chew holes in the furniture, carpet, and anything else that they can lay their teeth into.

And if this isn't bad enough, a hamster once escaped while travelling home from the pet shop in a car, and his owners could not find him. They had to resort to getting a garage to strip the car. They even called the fire brigade to help in the search with heat-seeking camera equipment. The total cost of the search was 253 times the cost of the missing hamster!

Another hamster escaped in the car while his owner was playing with him on the backseat. The hamster could not be found. The following morning, when the car failed to start, it was taken to the garage, where mechanics unsuccessfully tried to locate the missing hamster. The hamster was finally found 13 days later running around the floor of the garage workshop, but not until after he had succeeded in chewing through all the car's main wires.

It's not just the car that hamsters can damage—another hamster escaped, chewed through an electric cable, and set fire to the house.

One runaway hamster was believed dead until he was found two-and-a-half years later, alive and well and living in the sofa! During this time, the family had even moved twice. So be sure to keep cage doors firmly shut and supervise a hamster while out of the cage at all times. Not doing so can prove to be very costly!

Beware—a hamster doesn't have to escape to cause damage. One hamster set fire to his owner's house by running so fast on his wheel that the friction caused the hamster's bedding to catch fire, which in turn set fire to the nearby curtains. This is a freak occurrence, but it does show that careful consideration should be given to the location of the cage.

However, not all hamsters cause such havoc, and one hamster even saved his owners from fire rather than created it. On sensing smoke, the hamster warned his owners of an electrical fire that had started nearby by making lots of noise and waking the owners. The owners escaped the fire but forgot to take the hamster! Luckily, the hamster somehow managed to escape from his cage and was found ten days later within a wall frame of the fire-damaged house.

weeks of age, serious fighting, even resulting in death, will occur. Therefore, if you are considering buying more than one hamster, it is important to keep this fact in mind.

The dwarf species and the Chinese hamster are all sociable with their own kind and so can be kept in pairs or groups in one cage. However, they are best introduced at a young age. Introducing a new hamster to an older one is often not successful. The different species should not be mixed, because each species has a very different character from the others and they do not inhabit the same areas in the wild. Mixing the species is thus unnatural and results in a highly stressful environment for all, even if no fighting occurs.

Syrian hamsters must be housed separately, even if they are caged together at the pet store. Serious fighting will occur if Syrian hamsters are forced to share their "territory."

Equipment

Cages

The main piece of equipment required for the keeping of hamsters is a cage. There are cages designed specifically for hamsters or small rodents in pet stores, and the variety available is vast.

The basic form of hamster cage consists of a plastic base with the sides and top made of rigid wire. Some consist of only one level, while others may have several levels with ladders providing access to each level. These cages are relatively cheap, durable, and easy to clean. The top part clips to the base and allows for easy removal when cleaning the cage or handling the hamster. However, this type of cage does not offer protection from drafts, and unless the base is over two inches (four centimeters) in height, there is a tendency for the hamster to kick the floor covering through the bars when attempting to dig or burrow. A cage with bars on any of the floor surfaces is not ideal, because the hamster's feet can easily slip through when he runs, causing injury. If you use this standard type of cage for dwarf hamsters, the metal bars must be spaced no further than a quarter-inch (half a centimeter) apart to prevent escapes.

A popular but more expensive type of cage consists of enclosed plastic compartments linked by tubes. This type of cage comes with lots of modular options, and it does have the advantage of keeping the floor covering in the cage and offering protection from drafts to the hamster. However, these cages are not so easy to take apart to clean or gain access to the hamster.

It is important if you buy this type of cage that one compartment is at least 12 in x 12 in (30 cm x 30 cm) to give the hamster an adequate area in

J is for Judging—Carried out at hamster shows. Each hamster is judged and awarded points before a winner is determined.

which he can exercise freely. It is also important that the width of the tubes is carefully considered, because large, full-grown Syrian hamsters may not move freely through small tubes. Generally, the tubes provided are adequate for the dwarf species, although these smaller species may have problems climbing vertical tubes. However, the addition of a small ladder within the vertical tube easily overcomes this problem. Any tubes should be at least 2 3/4 in (7 cm) in width to accommodate a full-grown Syrian hamster without difficulty.

Another type of cage that is becoming more widely available is similar to a plastic aquarium with a ventilated plastic lid. These are lightweight, easily cleaned, and reasonably priced. However, it is important that the lid is out of reach of the hamster, because they are able to chew through the ventilated lid fairly easily, making a hole large enough for an escape.

Aquariums are also a popular choice as a hamster cage. These offer protection from drafts, prevent the floor covering from being kicked out, and are reasonably priced but not so easy to clean or move due to their weight. Any aquarium should include a ventilated lid. This will prevent anything from being accidentally dropped into the aquarium and injuring the hamster and

The basic hamster cage consists of a plastic base with wire sides and top. Hamster starter kits sold in pet shops provide all the equipment that you'll need for your new pet.

Capturing an Escaped Hamster

An escaped hamster often does not travel far from his cage, so shut all doors to the room first to prevent further wandering.

The hamster is most likely hiding somewhere dark and safe, so if an initial search is not successful, a humane trap can be built as follows:

1. Place a bucket or wastebasket in the room.

2. Place some paper bedding in the bucket or basket along with a piece of apple or other favorite hamster treat.

3. Build some steps up the outside of the bucket or basket using books or something similar that the hamster will be able to climb.

4. Leave some small pieces of food on some of the steps, just enough to entice the hamster to climb higher.

5. Leave overnight.

When he is active at night, the hamster should smell the food on the steps and the apple in the bucket/basket. He should then climb the steps and fall into the bucket or basket and be unable to escape, ready for discovery in the morning. If this is not successful on the first night, the trap should be left the following night.

will prevent the hamster from escaping. Don't be fooled into thinking that the sides of an aquarium are too tall for the hamster to escape—they are able to push wood shavings into a corner, providing a good platform for escaping.

Whatever cage is provided, it is important that the total floor space be at least 16 in x 12 in (40 cm x 30 cm), and preferably larger. The hamster will spend the majority of his time in his cage, so it is important that careful consideration be given to the selection to ensure that the hamster is provided with a suitable environment. As a rule, the larger the cage, the better.

Floor Covering

Wood shavings are the best form of floor covering for the cage. They provide an absorbent, non-slip surface for the hamster to move around on. The hamster will also enjoy digging and burrowing in the wood shavings.

Wood shavings made from cedar are unsuitable, because they can cause severe reactions in hamsters, such as respiratory inflammation. Cedar shavings can be distinguished by their red tint. Pine shavings, aspen shavings, or shavings made from wood pulp are all suitable floor coverings.

K **is for Kale**–A vegetable that many hamsters enjoy.

Nesting Material

Although the dwarf species will happily pile the wood shavings in a corner in order to build a nest, it is not so easy for a Syrian hamster to build his large nest with wood shavings alone. In any case, all species will appreciate some nesting material. There are various nesting and bedding materials sold in pet stores, but beware, because not all are safe for small animals.

Generally, nesting material that cannot be dissolved in water should be considered unsuitable, because if the hamster eats it, it could cause a stomach blockage leading to death. Nesting material from manmade fibers can result in the fibers being wrapped around limbs, causing severe injury. By far the best and safest nesting material is plain shredded paper—this is easily torn and dissolves if eaten, causing no harm to the hamster.

Water Bottle

A water bottle is required to allow the hamster to have constant access to clean water. There are many types of bottles available made from either glass or plastic, with a metal delivery tube. The types with a ball bearing in the delivery tube are less inclined to leak than those without.

Food Dish

A food dish is not essential, although many pet stores sell them. Your hamster will just as happily retrieve food from the floor of the cage, and it is actually more natural and stimulating for him to do so.

If a food dish is provided, it should be ceramic and not plastic. Plastic dishes are easily knocked over, which could result in a young hamster becoming trapped or injured.

A plastic aquarium with a ventilated lid is a popular alternative to the traditional wire cage.

Sunflower seeds, grain, rolled oats, corn, and alfalfa make good dietary supplements or can be offered as treats.

Exercise Wheel

Many cages are sold complete with an exercise wheel, while others are not. However, it is possible to buy stand-alone wheels that can be added to any cage. A wheel is a useful addition to a hamster's cage, because it provides an easy form of exercise for the hamster. Keep in mind that in the wild, a hamster may travel several miles in one night foraging for food, so exercise is natural for them.

Any exercise wheel should have a solid back and a solid running surface. Wheels with rungs allow the hamster's leg to slip through. If this occurs while the hamster is running, it can break the limb. Also, some hamsters have stuck their heads through the back of the wheel while running, with serious consequences.

Hamster Food

A hamster's basic diet consists of grains, cereals, and nuts, and there are a variety of different hamster diets available in pet stores. These are designed to meet the special dietary requirements of a hamster. Mixes designed for other animals should not be fed to hamsters, because they have been formulated to meet the requirements of another animal, which may not be the same as that of a hamster. They may also contain ingredients that

L **is for Laboratory**—Hamsters were originally kept and bred as laboratory animals before becoming the popular pet that they are today.

A ceramic food dish is not essential, but many hamster owners provide them. Your pet will also happily retrieve food from the floor of the cage.

are unsuitable for or toxic to hamsters. There is more information on feeding later on in this chapter.

Optional Equipment

A wide variety of additional equipment sold in pet stores can be placed in a hamster's cage to provide extra stimulation. Remember, the cage is where the hamster will spend the majority of his time, so the more stimulation available, the better.

Nesting houses or boxes provide an enclosed space for the hamster to sleep in and help to make him feel secure, offering a protection similar to his burrow in the wild. However, it is best to remove the lid from any nesting house or box, because once it is filled with nesting material and a sleeping hamster, condensation can become a problem.

Tubes may be placed inside the cage, and these provide good hiding places for the hamster and give him something to explore and climb on.

There are a number of "climbing frames" available in pet stores, and these provide the

Homemade Cages

A variety of homemade cages may be built to accommodate hamsters.

A large plastic storage container works just as well as a plastic aquarium but should have a wire top added to ensure that nothing is accidentally dropped in the cage and to prevent the hamster from escaping. Make sure the lid is well ventilated!

For the do-it-yourself enthusiast, cages may be made using wood and thick wire mesh, but the edges need protection against gnawing from the hamster. Regular cleaning is required, because urine soaks into wood. This is less of a problem if laminated wood is used. Plexiglas can also be added to provide a window on one side of the cage.

An aquarium can be made more interesting by adding wood shelves, providing different levels, or adding homemade wooden climbing frames.

A water bottle is a mandatory cage accessory. This hamster's water is tinted yellow with a liquid vitamin supplement.

hamster with something to explore and climb over, helping him to develop his muscles and balance. However, in a standard wire cage, hamsters will use the bars on the sides and top of the cage to show off their acrobatic abilities.

M is for **Mealworms**–A live treat enjoyed by many hamsters but not so popular with many of their owners.

It is important that any tubes, nesting houses, or climbing frames have holes, windows, and doorways large enough for the hamster to move through comfortably. If these are too small, the hamster may get stuck, and it should not be assumed that a hamster will "know better" than to try and squeeze through a hole that is obviously too small.

There are also toys for sale, such as hamster exercise balls. The hamster is placed inside the ball and can roll it around the floor. This is a safe way for the hamster to move about without fear of escape or injury. However, even when placed in a ball, the hamster should be supervised—hamsters have been known to break the ball apart and escape, take a bumpy ride down stairs, or even roll the ball outside and down the road through an open door. Although many hamsters seem to enjoy running around in these balls, not all hamsters do, so if your hamster seems unhappy, remove him from the ball. No hamster should be placed in an exercise ball for more than 20 minutes at a time, because the hamster has no access to water, and in an effort to try and get out of the ball (most often by running), can become exhausted.

A hamster's basic diet consists of grains, cereals, and nuts. Premixed hamster formulas are sold at pet stores.

Preparing the Cage

It is always best to prepare the cage before buying the hamster. The hamster can then be placed in the prepared cage as soon as you bring him home.

The cage should be prepared by lining all floors of the cage with a thick layer of wood shavings. Nesting material should be placed in a corner of the cage, in the sleeping compartment, or in the box.

Fill the water bottle with water and attach it to the side of the cage at a height that the hamster will be able to reach. Check that the water bottle is working correctly by running a finger over the end of the delivery tube. If you don't feel any water, squeezing the bottle will sometimes remove any air blockage. If the water bottle leaks or fails to deliver water, obtain a replacement bottle before buying the hamster.

Place a handful of hamster food either in a food dish within the cage or scattered on the floor of the cage.

Finally, place the cage in a room of fairly constant temperature, away from direct sunlight, radiators, and drafts, and out of the way of any pets that may attempt to harm the hamster.

Selecting a Hamster

A hamster may either be obtained from a pet store or directly from a breeder. Although obtaining a hamster from a breeder is preferable because you can see the parents, know the exact date of birth, and be assured that the hamsters have been regularly handled, it can often be difficult to locate breeders. Therefore, most pet hamsters are obtained from pet stores.

An exercise wheel for a hamster should have a solid back and running surface for safety's sake.

It is important to obtain a hamster from a store that is knowledgeable about them and, at the very least, is able to sex them and ensure that the males and females are kept in separate cages and that the females have not accidentally become pregnant.

Although some may think that buying a pregnant hamster is appealing, remember that hamsters of a young age are still growing themselves and are often not mature enough to cope with motherhood. An early pregnancy can result in many problems. Also, it is best not to disturb or handle the mother while she is still nursing, so handling the hamster will have to wait.

In all species of hamster, males are generally a little calmer than females, but any hamster will usually become

Many hamsters enjoy supervised 20-minute "outings" in exercise balls.

Homemade Cage Accessories

PVC drainage tubes make ideal nesting areas or tunnels for hamsters.

Shredded toilet paper or paper towel is safe, inexpensive nesting material.

Cotton reels make good toys for a hamster to gnaw on.

Children's interlocking blocks may be used to build a climbing frame for a hamster.

Cardboard toilet roll tubes are fun for hamsters—great for exploration and for tearing to shreds. A tube may be hung above the ground (not too high) using string, providing the hamster with an interesting tube to explore and climb on.

very tame with careful and regular handling.

When choosing a hamster, examine all hamsters in a cage carefully for signs of illness, such as a runny nose, runny eyes, thin body, wet or dirty bottom, ruffled hair, and lethargy. Although hamsters are asleep during the day, when they are awake, they should be bright and alert. If any hamster in a cage looks unwell, it is best to choose one from another cage and maybe even another store. Many illnesses are contagious, so one ill hamster in a cage means a high risk that others will also be ill or become ill.

Once you find a hamster that appeals to you, it is best to ask to handle him before buying. This will allow a closer inspection for health and an assessment of his temperament. The hamster's body should feel firm, the hamster should be bright and alert, and he should be clean. Any nervousness can be cured, but aggression is harder to deal with.

A new hamster will be very nervous when he first arrives in his new home. A couple of days of peace and quiet will help him settle in.

Going Home

The pet store will usually provide a cardboard container for the hamster's trip home. These are fine for short journeys but unsuitable for long journeys, because the hamster can easily chew his way out. Always check that the air holes are punched through and ensure they are not covered up while travelling.

For longer journeys, small plastic ventilated pet carriers may be purchased in pet stores, and these are ideal carriers for the trip home. These are also useful if the hamster has to go to the vet.

Arrival

On arrival home, immediately place the hamster in his new cage. The hamster is likely to be extremely nervous, having just traveled and arrived in a totally new environment. To enable the hamster to feel more confident and secure in his new home, it is best to leave him alone for a couple of days, apart from placing food in the cage. The hamster will soon become familiar with all the new smells and sounds and learn that he has nothing to fear.

Many new hamsters will frantically run around and dig for the first few days in their new cage and then spend the next few days resting from all the exertion.

> **N is for Nocturnal**—Hamsters sleep during the day and wake at dusk, becoming active during the evening and night.

Handling

After allowing a few days of peace for the hamster to adjust to the new environment, you can start to introduce yourself to your hamster by speaking to him. Hamsters do become used to their owner's voice and learn to accept this as a form of comfort.

Feeding the hamster a treat from your hand will introduce him to your hand and give the hamster a chance to become familiar with your smell. Progressing to stroking the hamster gently will get him used to the feeling of your hand against his body.

Once your hamster seems more confident in his new home and comfortable with your presence, you can progress to handling. It is always best to remove the top of the cage so that the hamster is easily accessible and you are able to pick him up by scooping him up in both hands.

Once the hamster is out of the cage, it is best to sit so that your hamster will not fall far if he jumps. Facing the hamster toward you is safer than facing him away from you, because there is no chance that he could jump and land on the floor where he may injure himself or escape.

It should be remembered that a hamster's eyesight is very poor, so sudden movements are likely to frighten him.

Feeding

A good basic hamster mix should form the main part of the hamster's diet. There are also rodent or hamster pellets available in pet stores, and although they meet the nutritional needs of hamsters, they do not offer the hamster much variety. If you buy rodent or hamster pellets, it is best to add some hamster mix to it to add variety to the basic diet.

It is also safe to feed a variety of other foods to hamsters, but these should only be fed as treats and should not form the main part of the diet. Any soft foods—for example, fruit and vegetables—

Always handle a potential pet such as this Chinese hamster before making your purchase. This will allow a closer inspection for health and will help you assess his temperament.

should be introduced to the hamster gradually in small amounts, because too much too soon can cause diarrhea. The amount of soft food fed may be gradually increased as long as the hamster shows no sign of diarrhea.

Some fruits and vegetables that are safe to feed are cabbage, carrot, apple, banana, broccoli, peas, blackberries, corn, swede, cauliflower leaves and stalks, celery, blueberries, cucumber, strawberries, cress, pear, kale, watercress, turnip, grapes, melon, and cooked potato.

> **O is for Oats**—One of the main ingredients of a basic hamster mix.

Fruit and vegetables that should not be fed are tomato leaves, onion, raw potato, potato tops, and rhubarb—these are all poisonous to hamsters.

Although lettuce may be given to hamsters, it has very little nutritional value, and too much over a period of time may cause liver problems.

Herbs and plants that may be given include parsley, groundsel, clover, dandelion, dock, and mint.

Other foods that may be fed as treats include cooked fish and meat, tofu, bread and toast, unsweetened cereals, currants, raisins, and scrambled or boiled egg. Mealworms and crickets may also be fed, and many hamsters relish them, but not every owner is willing to provide live foods.

There are also a variety of hamster treats sold in pet stores, many consisting of grains bound together by honey. These provide a good treat for the hamster, but too many can be fattening, so they should only be given occasionally. There are also chocolate drops, fruit drops, and yogurt drops available in pet stores, and most hamsters love them.

Treats for hamsters are sold in pet stores and come in a wide variety of sizes and flavors.

Chocolate that is made for human consumption should not be fed to hamsters because it is toxic—only chocolate drops specifically designed for hamsters or small rodents should be used, because these contain different ingredients that are safe for hamsters. Candy is also a no-no, because it can be dangerous to hamsters.

Feeding Time

Hamsters are nocturnal, so it is best to feed them in the early evening when they will be awake. Although food is plentiful in captivity, the natural instinct to hoard food remains, so a hamster will collect food to place in his food store. Although storing

Dried alfalfa and other vegetable foods are excellent supplements to a hamster's basic diet.

dry food usually causes no problems, moist food may start to rot if the hamster tries to stash it away. Because of this, the hamster should only be fed the amount of moist food that he can eat in one evening.

Care

Caring for a hamster is relatively easy. They require regular feeding, constant access to water, a clean environment, and treatment when they are ill.

Check the water bottle and refill it regularly, and feed the hamster in the evening. Hamsters eat relatively little, so only a small handful of food is required each day. However, due to their habit of storing food, it is not necessary to feed them every evening, and a large quantity of food can be placed in the cage every two or three days.

Clean the cage once a week by throwing away all old wood shavings, dirty bedding, and stored food. Wash the cage with a weak dishwashing solution followed by thorough rinsing or a disinfectant designed for small animal cages. If there is nothing available to place the hamster in while cleaning the cage, the hamster may be safely placed in the bathtub—this will keep the hamster safe and out of mischief while the cage is being cleaned. Make sure to close the bathtub drain!

Once the cage is clean and dry, set it up as usual and return the hamster. He is likely to spend some time inspecting the cage after cleaning—digging at the wood shavings, and rubbing himself or rolling around in order to lay his scent down in the clean cage before settling down.

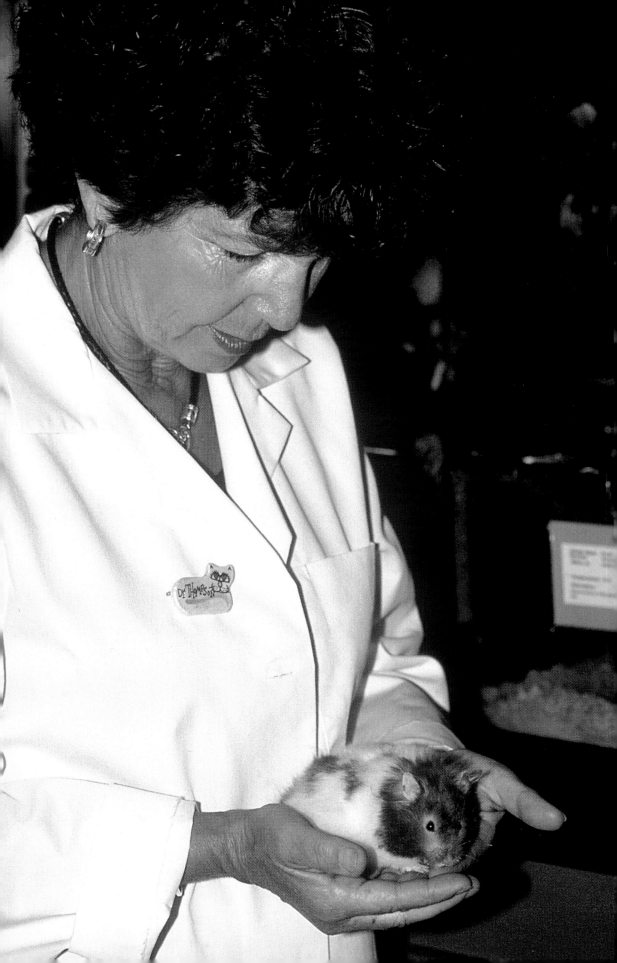

Health

Even with the best care and a regular routine, any hamster may get sick from time to time. Their small size means that illness can cause quick deterioration, so a hamster that shows any sign of poor health should be treated without delay.

Although it may be cheaper to leave the hamster untreated when he is sick and replace him with another hamster, it is a responsible pet owner's duty to care for the animal. Taking on a pet is a commitment—this means financial responsibility, not just time and general care.

Although many hamsters go through life without illness, it is inevitable that some will become sick. Some of the more common illnesses are detailed in this chapter.

Hamsters store food temporarily in their cheek pouches. If they are not emptied completely, the cheek pouches may become impacted.

Overcrowding and stress can quickly foster disease. Never purchase a hamster from a cage where even one other hamster is sick.

Abscess

An abscess normally occurs when a bite or other wound becomes infected, causing pus to build up under the skin. This can usually be seen as a lump that forms on the hamster and is easily treated by a vet, who can drain the pus and prescribe antibiotics to treat the infection.

Tumors and Cancers

Although tumors and cancers are more common in older hamsters, they can develop occasionally in young hamsters.

The first sign is often a hard lump that dramatically increases in size. These can often be surgically removed, and although there is a risk to the hamster's life from the operation and anesthesia, the majority of hamsters come through this type of surgery successfully. However, the sooner veterinary advice is sought, the greater the chance of successful removal.

> **P** **is for Pups**—The name often used to refer to baby hamsters.

Bladder/Kidney Infections

A bladder or kidney infection will cause the hamster to drink and urinate excessively. Blood may sometimes be seen in the urine and the hamster may appear to be in pain when urinating. Such infections are often easily treated with antibiotics prescribed by a vet.

Colds

The signs of a cold in a hamster are much the same as in humans—sneezing, runny nose, and runny eyes. Minor colds can usually be remedied by just placing the hamster in a warmer room for a few days. However, minor colds can very quickly turn into bronchitis or pneumonia, so veterinary treatment is advisable if there is cause for concern.

Constipation

A lack of droppings in the cage, sometimes with signs of straining by the hamster, is a symptom of constipation. Often this can be remedied by simply feeding the hamster some soft foods such as fruit and vegetables, but if this does not resolve the problem, the hamster should be taken to a vet. Constipation can be caused by a stomach blockage and so can ultimately be very serious.

Hamster Health Check
Does your hamster pass the test?

• Eyes are clean and bright with no signs of cloudiness or stickiness

• Ears are clean and not flaky

• Body feels firm and the hamster has not lost weight

• Hamster's droppings are dry and dark in color

• Hamster is active and alert when awake—ears are erect and he is ready to explore and play

• Teeth are not overgrown and do not prevent the hamster from shutting his mouth

• Fur is thick, shiny, and clean

A sudden change in diet is the most frequent cause of diarrhea.

Acrobatic play sessions can sometimes result in injured hamsters. Broken limbs must be allowed to heal naturally, because a cast is impractical.

Diarrhea

The most common cause of diarrhea in a hamster is a sudden change of diet or the feeding of too much soft food. The droppings are soft, watery, and light in color, and the hamster may be wet or messy around his bottom.

The hamster with diarrhea should be given a dry diet only along with fresh water, but if he has not recovered within a day or two, it is wise to seek veterinary advice, because the diarrhea could be a symptom of something more serious.

Wet Tail

This is a highly infectious and fatal disease in hamsters that is caused by a bacterial infection or imbalance of bacteria in the stomach. The most common cause of wet tail is stress. For this reason, it is important to allow the hamster time to settle when first arriving home, because this will help to keep stress to a minimum.

Q is for Quadruped–A four-legged animal like the hamster.

The symptoms include extreme diarrhea resulting in wetness and dirtiness around the bottom and the tail, giving the disease its name. The diarrhea is accompanied by a strong, unpleasant smell, and the hamster is extremely lethargic. This condition should not be confused with regular diarrhea.

The disease can act quickly, resulting in the hamster becoming dehydrated, and can be fatal in just a few days. There are over-the-counter medicines for wet tail that are sold in pet stores, but these are not as effective as full veterinary treatment. Given the seriousness of the disease, any hamster suffering from wet tail should be taken to the veterinarian immediately.

Broken Limbs

These usually occur as a result of an accident. The hamster may have fallen or jumped and landed awkwardly. It is not possible to put a plaster cast on a hamster because they are so small and would chew on it anyway. Therefore, the limb must be allowed to heal naturally. The removal of the wheel will help to keep exercise at a minimum while the limb heals, and if possible, the hamster should be placed in an aquarium or similar cage to prevent climbing. A high-calcium diet will also help the limb to repair.

Eye Problems

From time to time, a hamster may develop a minor eye problem. This may be caused by dust in the wood shavings or the hamster being placed in a draft. Older hamsters seem more prone to eye problems than young hamsters. The hamster's eyes may be sticky or remain shut, or they may be cloudy in appearance. Bathing the eye twice daily with a boric acid solution made by boiling and then cooling a cup of water and adding a teaspoon of boric acid powder can easily cure most eye problems.

Eye problems in hamsters sometimes result when a sharp piece of bedding injures the eye.

Fur Loss

During his life, a hamster will molt occasionally, and the fur may seem thinner at times. Older hamsters may develop some baldness around the belly and hips, but provided the skin appears normal, this is usually nothing to worry

R **is for Rodentia**—The scientific order of animals to which hamsters belong.

about. However, large patches of fur loss are usually a cause for concern.

Fur loss can be treated with brewer's yeast. Crush a tablet and sprinkle it over the hamster's food each day, reducing the amount once the fur has started to regrow. However, this will only help the fur to regrow. If the loss is due to skin irritation, brewer's yeast does nothing to alleviate the actual problem.

Widespread fur loss, or fur loss accompanied by skin irritation or flakiness, should be referred to a vet.

Mites

Mites in hamsters usually occur through transfer from other animals or infected hay. The hamster will scratch excessively and may develop fur loss. The mites may also be visible on close inspection.

A mite infestation can develop into mange, a condition that causes the skin to become flaky, accompanied by fur loss on the back of the hamster. The hamster may also develop scabs around the nose, ears, and genitals.

An anti-mite spray designed for small animals or caged birds is often effective against minor cases of mites when it is sprayed around the cage and over the hamster, being sure to shield the

A hamster that is allowed to exercise outdoors may pick up mites and other parasites. However, these are rare in hamsters that are always kept indoors.

The teeth of a hamster grow continuously, which is why it is so important for them to gnaw on hard surfaces.

hamster's face. However, serious and prolonged cases of mites or any signs of mange require veterinary attention.

Heat Stroke

When a hamster becomes too hot, he lies motionless on his stomach and often will tremble if touched. In minor cases, the hamster can be made more comfortable by moving him to a cooler room or placing a fan in the room facing away from the hamster but circulating the air. Otherwise, a fine mist of water can be sprayed over the hamster to cool him down. However, if the hamster does not respond within a few minutes, urgent veterinary advice may be needed.

Broken or Overgrown Teeth

A hamster's teeth are always growing, and the natural instinct of a hamster to gnaw is usually enough to prevent them from overgrowing.

However, particularly in older hamsters, one tooth may become broken, leaving the opposite tooth with nothing to grind against, or the teeth may begin to grow crooked, resulting in a similar problem. In such cases, the remaining teeth may become too long and prevent the hamster from closing his mouth.

The teeth can be clipped, but this needs to be done carefully, avoiding cutting the hamster's cheeks or tongue, and so is best done by a vet. If the hamster's teeth are growing crooked, the hamster may require regular teeth clipping.

Breeding Hamsters

The decision to breed hamsters should not be undertaken without a lot of thought beforehand. It is unlikely that you would want to keep all the babies, so plans first need to be made for the excess hamsters that will be created. It is no good to hope that homes can be found for them after the fact. Homes should be located before breeding ever takes place.

Local pet shops may be willing to take the hamsters that you do not intend to keep, but many will not because they have regular suppliers. It is best to approach them before breeding.

Syrian Hamsters

Because Syrian hamsters are solitary animals, breeding them is rather complicated. It is necessary to

When a female is in season, firmly stroke her back toward her tail. If the female freezes with her tail in the air, she is ready to accept a male.

Plenty of nesting material should be made available to the pregnant hamster a few days before the birth.

put the male and female together on the evening that the female is in season, which is the only time she will accept the advances of the male.

The best age to breed from a female for the first time is when she is four to six months of age. This enables her to complete her own development before undertaking the strain of raising a family.

A female usually comes into season every four days during the evening and is often more active than usual at this time. To establish whether a female is in season, firmly stroke her back toward her tail. If the female freezes motionless, with her belly pressed to the floor and tail in the air, she is ready to accept a male. If she chatters her teeth (a sign of annoyance) and continues to move around, she is not in season.

When a female is found to be in season, she can be placed with the male or they can be introduced on neutral ground. The male should never be placed in the female's cage, because she will defend her territory and attack him even when in season.

It is always a good idea to have something handy that can be used to separate the two hamsters if they start fighting—a pen or ruler makes a useful tool to push in between two fighting hamsters to separate them.

S is for Solitary/Social Behavior– Syrian hamsters like the solitary life, while dwarf hamsters are sociable and live happily in pairs or groups.

Some males, particularly young ones, may have a problem realizing what is expected of them, but after a while they usually get the idea. The male will mount and dismount several times during mating, washing himself each time. It is best to allow the mating to continue for at least 20 minutes unless either hamster gets annoyed beforehand. Once mating has taken place, the hamsters can be returned to their cages.

The gestation period of a Syrian hamster is 16 days. During the 16 days after mating, the female's nipples will become more prominent, and she will start to swell around her hips. It is important that the female be provided with plenty of food during this time, and additional foods that are high in protein will also help her through her pregnancy.

Two days before the expected birth, clean the cage and provide plenty of nesting material so that the female can prepare for the birth. The female should be disturbed as little as possible at this time. The female will give birth to the babies one at a time with a short interval between each birth, and some blood will be discharged during the birth.

The female may give birth in the nest or while in another area of the cage. However, this does not normally cause a problem, and she will either move the babies to the nest as she gives birth to each one or move them to the nest once birthing is complete.

The female should continue to be provided with plenty of food and high-protein foods while she

Population Explosion

The average litter size for a Syrian hamster is 8, but the largest recorded litter consisted of 26 babies.

The average litter of Dwarf Hamsters is 4 to 6, but the largest litter consisted of 14 babies.

Dwarf Hamsters kept together can breed at 3-week intervals, and a single female can have up to 18 litters in her lifetime.

Breeding hamsters is not something that should be undertaken casually!

When the babies are two weeks old like these little hamsters, it is safe to disturb the nest and touch the babies.

These hamsters are five weeks of age. They are just about ready to find new homes.

is nursing the babies and should be disturbed as little as possible. It is important that the nest is not disturbed or the cage cleaned for two weeks after the birth.

Once the babies are two weeks of age, it is safe to disturb the nest and touch the babies without fear of the mother rejecting them. At this point, the cage may be cleaned.

By the time the babies are three to four weeks of age, they are fully weaned and may be removed from the mother. The babies are also becoming sexually mature, so the male babies should be placed in a separate cage from the females.

By the time the babies are five or six weeks of age, they will have become confident enough to cope with being moved to a new environment and may go to the pet shop to be sold or go directly to their new homes.

Dwarf Hamsters and Chinese Hamsters

Because dwarf hamsters and Chinese hamsters are sociable with their own kind, breeding is a simple affair. Males and females may be kept together in pairs or groups, and breeding will occur naturally once they become sexually mature. This is usually around two to four months of age, or in the case of Roborovski hamsters, in the spring of the year following the birth of the female.

The pair or group can remain together during pregnancy and nursing, and other members of the pair or group will help to raise the young.

T is for Teddy Bear—Another name commonly given to the long-haired Syrian hamster.

The babies are born at short intervals, and the mother will place the babies in the nest. She may banish other members of the pair or group from

the nest for a few days, preferring to be on her own for a while, but will usually allow them to return after a while and help her to rear the young.

When breeding Chinese hamsters, it is particularly important to provide plenty of hiding spaces within the cage, because the females can become highly aggressive toward the males and other females in the cage during pregnancy and the early stages of nursing.

The nest should not be disturbed or the cage cleaned until the babies are two weeks old, at which point they can be handled.

At three to four weeks of age, the babies can be removed from the mother if you do not intend to keep them. It is best to separate the males and females to avoid breeding. The mother may also have another litter at this time, because mating often takes place immediately after birth. For this reason, breeding dwarf hamsters requires careful consideration, because it is not unusual for litters to be produced at three-week intervals.

At two-and-a-half weeks old, these Campbells Russian babies are just beginning to explore their environment.

By the time the dwarf hamster babies are five to six weeks of age, they can go to their new homes.

This Campbells Russian hamster may banish other hamsters from her nest for a few days after the birth of her babies. After that, they will return to help her raise her young.

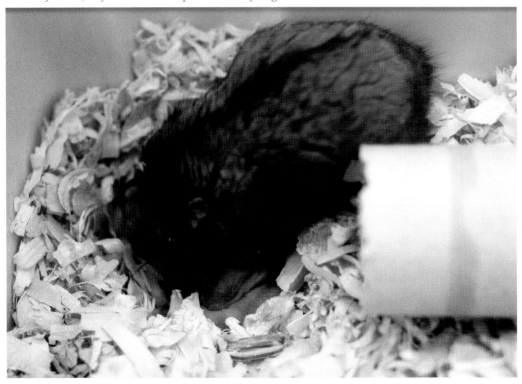

The Hamster Fancy and Hamster Shows

I n the 1940s, England became the first country to have a club set up for those interested in keeping hamsters. Today the UK has at least six clubs devoted entirely to hamsters and many other clubs devoted to rodents in general. At least three other European countries also have clubs devoted to hamsters or rodents.

There are comparatively few hamster clubs in the US, and many that do exist have only been formed fairly recently. However, with the increasing use of the Internet, US hamster owners are becoming aware of the sizable clubs in other countries. These "wired" US fanciers have begun to form more clubs in the US.

These clubs' main aim is to encourage the keeping of hamsters as pets and to educate hamster owners on their care. Most clubs publish a regular newsletter to serve this purpose. The clubs also provide hamster owners with access to experienced owners and breeders who can provide advice and other useful information.

Most clubs also hold regular hamster shows. Hamsters are judged against

A Cinnamon Satin Syrian hamster.

U **is for Underground**—In the wild, hamsters live in underground burrows consisting of many tunnels and chambers.

written standards of perfection. These standards and shows encourage breeders to breed quality hamsters that are good color examples. Breeders within the "hamster fancy," as it is known, have also been responsible for recognizing new genetic mutations as they have emerged and actively seeking to breed and establish them. Without the breeders within the hamster fancy, many of the colors seen today would not have survived and become well established.

Shows usually consist of a number of different classes for the different colors, coat types, and species. Hamsters are often shown in small containers referred to as "show pens." Each class is judged in turn, and each hamster is removed from the show pen for inspection by the judge. The judge assesses the hamsters for color and markings, size, quality of fur, and overall condition, and awards the hamster points accordingly. The hamster with the highest score is awarded first place for that class. At the end of the show, the hamster with the highest number of points across all the relevant classes is awarded with a Best in Show win.

A Dark Gray Syrian hamster.

Many hamsters found in pet stores will not meet the high standards required on a show bench, having been bred by breeders who have no interest in color, type, or other such qualities. However, that is not to say that a show winner cannot be found in a pet store, just that the chances are not high.

Most shows, however, do include a pets class for those with "average" pet hamsters. In these classes, the hamster is judged merely on his suitability as a pet and his general condition and health. These classes are an ideal way for a new hamster owner or new club member to become introduced to the world of showing.

A Golden Syrian hamster.

The hamster shows also act as a meeting place for breeders and hamster owners, providing a chance to meet other owners and breeders and learn more about hamsters, breeding, and showing. They also provide the pet owner with a chance to see and obtain some of the less common colors and varieties that are not usually seen in pet stores.

A Satin long-haired Golden hamster.

Colors and Varieties

Syrian Hamster

The natural coloring of the Syrian hamster in the wild is golden-brown, which is why it is sometimes referred to as the golden hamster. However, during the years it has been kept in captivity, a

A Light Gray Syrian hamster.

number of color, pattern, and coat mutations have occurred, and the combination of these has allowed still more colors to be developed.

Golden—The Golden is golden-brown over the back with dark gray roots, an ivory belly, black eyes, and gray ears. On the side of the cheeks, there is a black line that extends up toward the ears.

Cinnamon—The Cinnamon is ginger in color with blue-gray roots, an ivory belly, red eyes, and pale ears. Some Cinnamons may lack the brightness apparent in others.

Rust—The Rust is similar in color to the Cinnamon but has black eyes and gray ears. The coat is less bright than the Cinnamon and is a dull brownish-ginger with gray roots.

Dark-Eared White—The whole body is pure white and the eyes are red. The ears are gray and become darker with age.

Black-Eyed Cream—The whole body is cream to the roots and becomes a darker and brighter cream with age. The eyes are black and the ears dark gray.

Dark Gray—A rare but very attractive color. It is gray with dark gray roots, an ivory belly, and has a black line on each cheek extending up towards the ear. The eyes are black and the ears are dark gray.

Light Gray—Light gray in color with dark gray roots, an ivory belly, and a dark grayish-brown line on each cheek. The muzzle is distinctly cream-colored, the eyes are black, and the ears are dark gray.

Silver Gray—The closest of the grays to a Chinchilla gray. It is silver-gray in color with dark gray roots, an ivory belly, black eyes, and gray ears.

A Yellow Syrian hamster.

Black—Sometimes referred to as the "black bear," the Black Syrian hamster is jet black to the roots with white feet, black eyes, and gray ears.

Yellow—The back and sides are yellowy-cream in color with black tips. The eyes are black and the ears gray. Young Yellows may seem to be cream in color, but the color becomes richer and the hair tips darker with age.

Sable—Sometimes mistaken for Black, this hamster has black fur that is cream at the roots with distinctive cream

V is for Veterinarian—The person to visit if your hamster is sick.

rings around the eyes. As these hamsters get older, the black fur can change to a charcoal gray or very dark brown coloring.

Flesh-Eared White—The Flesh-Eared White is not a true Albino but what is known as a "synthetic Albino," being "manufactured" by combining the Dark-Eared White and Cinnamon. It has a pure white coat, red eyes, and pale ears.

W is for Wheel—Most hamsters love to use these to exercise and will run for many miles every night.

Red-Eyed Cream—The whole body is pinkish-cream to the roots, the eyes are red, and the ears are pale. The color becomes brighter with age, and the eyes darken to ruby red in color.

Mink—The body is a dull mid-brown in color with paler roots and pale rings around the eyes. The eyes are red and the ears are pale. The fur becomes a brighter orange-brown and the eyes a darker red with age.

Honey—The coat is a rich orange-cream in color to the roots with an ivory belly, red eyes, and pale ears.

A Red-Eyed Cream Syrian hamster.

Blonde—The Blonde is a creamy blonde in color with gray roots, an ivory belly, red eyes, and pale ears. It has a distinct rich cream muzzle.

Lilac—Lilac-gray in color with gray roots, an ivory belly, red eyes, and pale ears. Young lilacs are very attractive in color, but many develop a brown tint as they get older.

Smoke Pearl—The fur on the back is pale gray to the roots in color with black tips, the belly is ivory, the eyes are black, and the ears are gray.

Dove—The body is dove brown to the roots in color, the eyes are red, and the ears are pale. The eyes become darker with age.

Copper—The body is rich copper with paler roots, pale rings around the eyes, red eyes, and pale ears. The color becomes brighter with age, and the eyes become darker.

Black-Eyed Ivory—The body is off-white in color, the eyes are black, and the ears are gray.

Red-Eyed Ivory—The body is off-white in color, the eyes are red, and the ears are pale. The eyes often become darker with age.

A long-haired Sable Syrian hamster.

A Tortoiseshell-and-White Syrian hamster.

Chocolate (Sable)—The body is milk chocolate in color with paler roots, the eyes are black, and the ears are gray.

Chocolate (Black)—The body is dark chocolate brown to the roots in color with black eyes and gray ears. It has white feet.

Tortoiseshell—A bi-colored hamster achieved by combining Yellow with another color. Although it is possible to breed Tortoiseshells in a variety of colors, the most attractive is the Black Tortoiseshell—a hamster that is black with yellow patches. Introducing a white pattern produces a Tortoiseshell-and-White.

Banded—Banded is a white pattern that can be combined with any of the colors listed above. The pattern gives a pure white belly and a band of white across the center of the back. The white band may be incomplete and not meet in the middle of the back, or it may have spots of color in it.

Dominant Spot—This white pattern produces a hamster with a pure white belly. The back is white with colored spots. However, the spots may not be clearly defined or may be so large that little white is seen on the back. Dominant Spot hamsters often have a white

A Dominant Spot Syrian hamster.

blaze on the face, and the colored spots may be of any color.

Roan—Roan is another white pattern that may be produced in any color. The belly is pure white, and the back is white with colored hairs sprinkled throughout. The color is often concentrated around the head, and very little color may be present over the body.

Coat Length—The normal coat of the Syrian hamster is short, but over the years different coat mutations have occurred.

A Sable Roan Syrian hamster.

Long-Haired—The long-haired Syrian hamster is sometimes called a "teddy bear hamster." The females have shorter coats than the males. The coat is fluffy and the males can develop long tufts of hairs from the hips or around the bottom. Some males have long coats all over.

Rex—This is a rare variety. The coat is soft and curled upward, giving it a deep plush look on short-haired hamsters and a rather messy appearance on long-haired hamsters. A Rex is easily identified by the curly whiskers.

Satin—A Satin hamster has a very glossy coat.

Hairless—The hairless Syrian hamster is sometimes referred to as the "alien hamster." The body is completely hairless although the hamster may have whiskers.

X is for Xenophobia—The hatred of strangers. Hamsters are fiercely territorial and will attack other unfamiliar hamsters.

A normal-colored Dwarf Campbells Russian hamster.

Dwarf Campbells Russian Hamster

Normal—The normal coloring of the Dwarf Campbells Russian hamster is a mid-brownish-gray, with dark gray roots and a dark gray stripe running from the head, down the back toward the tail. The belly is ivory, the eyes are black, and the ears are gray.

Albino—The fur is pure white, the eyes are red, and the ears are pale.

Argente—The coloring is a rich ginger with blue-gray roots, a gray-brown line extending down the back with ivory belly, red eyes, and pale ears. However, many Argentes are pale in color, with the rich ginger diluted to almost cream in color and the dorsal line barely visible. Some breeders refer to the Argente as Cinnamon.

Black-Eyed Argente—Sometimes referred to as "sandy." The coloring is a dull ginger with gray roots, a gray-brown line extending down the back, ivory belly, black eyes, and gray ears.

Opal—A soft blue-gray with gray roots, with a soft gray line extending down the back. The belly is ivory, the eyes are black, and the ears are gray.

Black—A recent mutation that was imported into the US in 1999. The coat is black to the roots with a barely visible darker stripe down the back. The feet are white, the eyes black, and the ears gray.

Blue Fawn—The coloring on the back is ginger with a blue tint, blue-gray roots, and a soft gray-brown stripe extending from the head to the tail. The belly is ivory, the eyes red, and the ears pale.

Dove—The coat is dove-brown in color to the roots. The eyes are red and the ears are pale.

Mottled—The Mottled is a white pattern that can be combined with any color. The belly is pure white, and the patterning across the back can be very varied. Some hamsters have only a few white spots, a white collar, or a back that is mostly white with varying amounts of colored spots or

An Argente Dwarf Campbells Russian hamster.

An Opal Dwarf Campbells Russian hamster.

patches. Due to the variety of patterning that can be produced, the Mottled is sometimes referred to by other names such as Pied, Dominant Spot, Banded, and Collared.

Platinum—The Platinum combined with any color gives a silvered appearance. The belly is white, and the colored back has white hairs sprinkled through. The amount of white hairs on the back often increases with age.

Y is for Yogurt Drops—A treat enjoyed by hamsters and found in many pet stores.

Dilute Platinum (White)—The Dilute Platinum is pure white and can either have black eyes or red eyes. The ears are pale but may have dark spots or patches on them. The white coat may have a few colored hairs, particularly around the face.

Satin—The Satin has a shiny, "wet-look" coat and can be produced in any color.

Left: A Sapphire Winter White Russian hamster. Right: A Pearl Winter White Russian hamster.

Dwarf Winter White Russian Hamster

Normal—The normal coloring of the Dwarf Winter White Russian is darkish gray with darker gray roots and a jet-black stripe from the head to the tail. The belly is ivory, the eyes black, and the ears gray.

Sapphire—The coat is soft purple-gray in color with gray roots, with a soft gray stripe extending from the head toward the tail. The belly is ivory, the eyes black, and the ears gray.

Pearl—The coat is pure white, with colored hairs ticked through the back. The colored hairs tend to be more concentrated around the head and dorsal area. Some Pearls have so few colored hairs that only a few may be evident around the head.

Chinese Hamster

Normal—The normal coloring is chestnut

A Black Mottled Dwarf Campbells Russian hamster.

A normal-colored Chinese Hamster.

A normal-colored Roborovski hamster.

brown with dark gray roots and a dark brown stripe extending from the head to the tail. The belly is ivory, the eyes black, and the ears gray.

Dominant Spot—The Dominant Spot has a pure white belly and the back is white and brown. The amount of white on the back can vary among different hamsters.

Roborovski Hamster

Normal—The normal coloring of the Roborovski is sandy-gold with gray roots and a white belly. The Roborovski has no line extending down the back and has distinctive white "eyebrows" above the eyes. As yet, no other colors have occurred.

> **Z** **is for Zoology**—The study of animals, including hamsters.

Index

Photo Credits

Joan Balzarini, 18, 20, 40, 46

Isabelle Francais, 8, 23, 29, 31, 32, 36, 44

Michael Gilroy, 1, 13, 14, 22, 34, 57

Lorraine Hill, 9, 10, 11 T & B, 15, 19, 21, 27, 30, 33, 35, 37, 47, 49, 51, 52, 53 T & B, 54, 55, 56T, 58 T & B, 59 T & B, 60(all), 61 T & B, 62(all), 63(all)

Aimee Strickland, 16, 39, 50

John Tyson, 4, 5, 12, 17 T & B, 38, 41, 45, 48, 56B